Christmas Eve In Branksome Hall ..

[Quetting, Ellen D] [from old catalog]

Christmas Eve

IN

Branksome Hall

CHRISTMAS EVE

— IN —

Branksome Hall

" Sit with me by the homestead hearth,
And stretch the hands of memory forth,
To warm them at the wood-fire's blaze ! "
　　　　　　—*Whittier*.

NEW YORK :
J. W. PRATT, BOOK AND JOB PRINTER, 75 FULTON STREET.
1879.

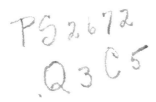

To my Mother,

THESE RECOLLECTIONS OF OUR EARLY HOME ARE

INSCRIBED BY HER LOVING CHILD,

ELLEN D. QUETTING.

Christmas Eve in Branksome Hall.

---+---

Blest Memory! whose silent flashes bright
    Illume the realm of mind ;
Give back the smile and glance of light
    In heart enshrined.

Blest Memory! whose lingering echoes sweet
    The rolling years prolong,
Give back like bugle-blast the voices of the past,
    And cheer my song.

Wrapped in sweet musings of the past,

 There rises on my sight

The scenes and home of other days

 In clear and vivid light.

How bright and gay the old hall looks!

 Who did the garlands weave?

It seems a green and leafy bower

 This merry Christmas Eve.

The doors are wreathed with mountain-ash,

 Glistening with berries bright;

The walls festooned with hemlock,

 With cross and star bedight.

This home in festal splendor,

 So dear to one and all;

Was christened by our uncle,

    Dear Frank, as " Branksome Hall."

The house was built of wood,

    As strong as any fort;

And was, for all the country 'round,

    The open, free resort.

The friend, the neighbor, welcome found ;

    The poor, the sick, forlorn ;

No rest the Doctor had from calls,

    From eve till dewy morn.

The wanderer found a downy bed,

    A rest from all his cares ;

He turned no man away, lest one

    Were " angel unawares."

The mistress of the mansion,

    True angel, friend and wife,

Bore with brave heart the burden

    With which her world was rife.

She nursed the sick, mourned with the sad,

    She clad the needy poor;

And none went empty-handed

    Who asked alms at her door.

The Doctor quoted Holy Writ

    His virtuous wife to praise,

Who in the path of life had walked

    Consistently always.

" Your mother is as good," said he,

    " As any saint of old;

" And she would never think of doing

"Their deeds in Scripture told."

Father and mother, sister and brother,

Are seated in the Hall.

This Christmas eve are gathered there

Ellen, George, Mary, all

Their friends—another Mary,

Ellen's great friend is here

(From a pretty village, miles away),

To taste the Christmas cheer.

Her open look and clear gray eyes

Have heart and good will won.

The beaming face and blooming youth

Are fair to look upon.

Here come our uncles, Ad. and Frank,
    Our mother's younger brothers,
With us as much at home, I ween,
    As any of the others.
Dear Ad., with heart like sound, good fruit,
    Which time more fully mellows,
By the whole village is esteemed
    "The Prince of all good fellows;"
And Frank! companion welcome ever,
    How paint thy social merits,
That make thy company to all
    Like good wine for the spirits?

What is thy humor, Frank, to-night?

   From memory's full treasures,

Wilt Shakespeare, Milton, Byron, Scott,

   Repeat in ample measures?

Or Virgil, Cicero, and Livy,

   With rapture so translate,

One feels the classic mind of old

   Thy genius well can mate.

Macauley, Webster, Clay, and Burke,

   With voice, and look, and tone;

Thou canst for hours their words repeat,

   As if they were thine own.

Wilt, in thy attitude and style,

   With Kean and Forrest vie,

And show the worthies of the town

   In matchless mimicry.

Thou know'st in lively wit and jest,

   And sprightly repartee,

In friendly bout to sally out

   In " goodlie companie."

Now come the Academy teachers,

   And neighbors with their dames,

And children in the sitting-room

   Play noisy, happy games.

As conversation now begins

   Its mingled busy hum,

A loud knock at the door is heard—

What visitor has come?

A figure, wrapped in snowy garb,

Chilled from a long, cold ride,

Is ushered in—he cannot stay—

'Tis messenger and guide.

On the lake shore, ten miles away,

By an unbroken road,

A child is sick—brooks no delay—

Must haste to the abode.

The Doctor must with him at once.

At duty's earnest call,

Our host and father turns straightway,

And passes from the Hall.

A quick good-bye—a backward glance

At cheerful home and light—
And speeding on at mercy's call,
   He vanishes in night;
And silence for a moment falls
   Upon the busy throng,
And sympathizing glances
   From eyes now pass along.
Our mother, trained in duty's path
   Unquestioning to walk,
With one brief sigh says quickly
   Kind words to link the talk.

"Come, Julia, tell some legend old
   Of Knights of high degree—

Of Lords and Ladies—Tournaments

    And deeds of chivalry!

Some stirring romance of old days,

    Or tender, moving lay,

Above the train of common thought—

    Befitting festal day."

JULIA'S STORY.

Baron Arnold Von Cöllen lay dying,

    And tossing and moaning in pain;

And the Lady Elizabeth's tears,

    And weeping, and sobbing, were vain.

The good Baron was of the Church
  A faithful and dutiful son,
But his ancestors in the dim past
  Were heretics—every one.

They fought with the Brandenburg army,
  With Gustavus Adolphus for might;
And many a rood of good land
  They won by stout arm in the fight.

When the thirty years' war was all over,
  The Barons Von Cöllen had store
Of worldly goods, land, and of gold—
  Could their children e'er want any more?

But time plays strange pranks in its course,
　　With whirlwind and battle full rife;
And, two centuries after, the broad lands
　　Had vanished in war, waste and strife.

The old crumbling ruin at Jülich,
　　Where the Baron lay dying to-day,
Looked down on the remnants of birthright—
　　Two lone, straggling villages gray.

The Baron now begged his sad wife
　　For Father Ignatius to send;
Fears, doubts and perplexities vexed him,
　　Consolation the Church could now lend.

Acolytes came with bell and with book,

    Chrismatorium with holy oil,

And bearing on high, cross and pyx

    The poor dying man to assoil.

The Jesuit brother came after—

    A monk gaunt with penance and fast—

With expression cold, austere and sad—

    Eyes with zeal and devotion o'ercast.

To the Father the Baron now said:

    "What penance can I, ere I die,

For the sake of my soul and the dead,

    Do, in God's name, for sweet Charity?"

" For the deeds of the past, my dear son,

   Thy ancestors many a year

Have inherited torments and pains

   In the regions the wicked now fear.

" Of thy goods, and thy houses and lands,

   Give the Church now no poor meagre dole;

And from pains, and from wrath and distress,

   In mercy, deliver each soul."

" Good Father, I have wife and child,

   To heart and affection most dear!"

" Thy wife St. Ursula's Abbess shall be;

   Thy son in the Holy Faith rear."

He guided the hand of the dying man.

The deed was done; and the Church's ban

Rested no longer on his race;

And a smile lit up the pallid face.

The monk now ended his holy function,

And the faithful man received the unction;

And the spark of life no longer fanned,

The Baron passed to a better land.

The Lady Elizabeth many a day

Lived in the walls of St. Ursula, gray;

And many a prayer and mass were said

For the son now living, and the Baron dead.

The brotherhood received the son

As a soul for the Church's bosom won;

But the fires of heresy were not dead,

And from the Jesuits he fled.

To a distant land his steps he turned,

And a fierce unrest within him burned.

Outcast, he wandered many a year,

And crossed to the Western Hemisphere.

By the Duke of Hesse to England sold,

With the Hessian ranks he fought for gold;

And like his ancestors, long dead,

By his strong arm he won his bread.

The Jesuit College, endowed with his lands,

For a century flourished in their hands;

And the lights are lit, and the mass is said,

O'er the faithful Arnold's escutcheoned bed;

But his recreant son, for heresy banned,

Lies buried unknown on a foreign strand.

No stone for his head, no mass for his soul,

And his name erased from memory's roll.

With kindly words, this ballad strange

   The patient listeners greet;

But the mother gravely and sadly says,

   "This tale is for our ears not meet."

And Julia answers, "I can naught change,

   What e'er your feelings be,

I narrate everything for truth,

    As it was told to me."

A tone of sadness pervades the Hall,

    And now one calls for a song.

Whose voice is in tune, young maidens?

    We wait—don't hesitate long.

Hettie, sing us the rhymes you have written,

    Although simple the ditty may be;

We will give to our friends a warm welcome—

    Let the chorus ring out cheerily.

She has a bad cold—Will. must join the refrain;

    She has sung nothing for—oh, ever so long.

But plucking up courage with ahem—'hem—

'hem—

She strikes up the tune, and sings us this song:

HETTIE'S SONG..

TUNE AULD LANG SYNE.

To Branksome Hall each honored guest,

Welcome and cheer to-night;

For you we've wreathed the walls about,

And hung the berries bright.

So, Merrie Christmas to our friends—

A Merrie Christmas, all!

May each be happy as a king

To-night, in Branksome Hall

For you the hearthstone high is piled;

   For you we sing our songs;

And they shall be of right good will

   That to the time belongs.

     So, Merrie Christmas to our friends, etc.

The star that o'er Judea's hills

   Rose the first Christmas night,

Has never yet returned again

   To dazzle human sight.

     So, Merrie Christmas to our friends, etc.

But myriad shapes in flame and gold

   As symbols now are seen;

And we have made a star for you
  Of shining evergreen.
    So, Merrie Christmas to our friends, etc.

All 'round the earth shall circle still,
  From eve to early morn,
The tidings of that glorious day
  On which our Lord was born.
    So, Merrie Christmas to our friends, etc.

The bells shall ring from belfries high,
  The chimes from each church tower;
And angel choirs shall chant their song
  When strikes the midnight hour.

Then let us keep this holiday
With peace, good will to all;
May each be happy as a king
To-night, in Branksome Hall.

Our mother lifts her hand, and says:
"In all our joy and mirth,
Let us recall in distant lands
One absent from our hearth.
Far, in the pleasant sunny South,
Are generous homes and free;
May one its circle ope' for him
In hospitality.
May our dear Lord, this festal night,

Keep him within his ken."
And every heart in silence there
    Answers a deep Amen.

I glance around, and see uncle Frank
    By the bright rays of the moon,
Through the half open door beyond the Hall,
    Like a goldsmith burnish a spoon.

The group around him merry grow
    At the story that comes after,
And at the end there follows now
    A hearty burst of laughter.

Aside, I propose to Mary to go

　　And visit the sitting-room,

To see what mischief the children do.

　　We open the door, and before us loom

Two tall ghosts spooking about.

　　The children shriek and laugh by turns,

Half in fear and half in doubt,

　　While the lamp, turned down, dimly burns.

Eva and Belle, each with a broom,

　　Wrapped in a sheet, with nose and eyes

Pinned on, stalk about from room to room.

　　(Oh, childhood! Oh, youth! How time flies!

I have played the same games,

　　And have had the same fears;

Laughed as merrily oft as any of you,

    And reaction has ended in tears).

Like sudden bursts of April showers

    That dim the glowing skies,

O'er-charged abundance spends its force—

    Refreshed all nature lies.

At our appearance, the children all

    Came running at full speed,

Glad to be rescued from their fears,

    In this their hour of need.

"Come, aunt," says Clayton, "tell a story—

    Let it be something good!

Tell us of good St. Nicholas,

    Or of bold Robin Hood."

THE AUNT'S STORY.

THE ORIGIN OF THE CHRISTMAS TREE.

'Twas the night before Christmas,
  Just ten years ago,
The icicles glittered
  Like diamonds in snow.
The man in the moon
  Took a peep o'er the wood,
And the evening star twinkled
  Near by where he stood;
And we knew 'twas the herald
  To prelude the morn
That should tell to the world

That the Christ-child was born.

Old Prancer and Dasher

  Champed their bits at the door,

While the sleigh stood behind

  With the driver before;

    And John, with his fur cap

And shag coat of brown,

Looked as if he 'd just come

  From an Esquimaux town.

The children were muffled

  In tippets and mittens,

And were tucked in the sleigh robes

  As snug as the kittens.

George, Walter and Philo,

Lucy, Mary and I

Had just said to our mothers

A parting good-bye.

Aunt Lucinda lived on

The great road to the East,

And here all the children

Expected a feast.

We plunged through the snow—

Hurrahed for the night—

Were ever young hearts

More joyous and light!

The dogs followed after

With hearty good-will;

Now behind—now before—

As we sped up the hill.

The bells jingled loud
   In the frosty night air;
And we joked, and we laughed,
   Without sorrow or care.

We passed the gnarled chestnut trees
   Of the dark woods;
By the thicket of hemlocks,
   All wrapped in white hoods.

From each cosy farm-house
   The glimmering light
Told of joy and good will
   And feasting to-night;
And the smoke from the chimneys

Seemed to us but a type

Of the ascending clouds

From St. Nicholas' pipe.

We passed by the country road,

Turned to the right,

And the lonely brick school-house

Appeared in our sight.

Here the wind had piled up

The snow banks so high,

'Twas a question to know,

Could we pass safely by?

We cry, here 's Mont Blanc!

Which we scale in a trice.

The horses step slow

On the glare of the ice.

We safely ascend

To the top of the knoll,

But descending, upset,

In the snow we all roll.

What a scramble, and shouting,

And laughter we raised!

One had thought for a truth

We were all somewhat crazed.

George alone cried aloud,

He had broken his nose;

But the rest of us only

Complained of our toes.

John righted the sleigh:

We were soon in again,

And he gave to old Prancer

And Dasher the rein,

And we soon came in sight

Of the cheering lamp-light,

That shone through the windows,

So beckoning and bright;

And through the great gate-way

We drove with a shout,

That brought both the man

And maid-servants out.

Our aunt at the window,

The rest at the door—

And we met such a greeting

As never before.

Up the great stone chimney
    The fiery flames leaped
From the back-log, and fore-stick,
    And pine knots, high heaped ;
And the gleams on the floor,
    And the gleams on the wall
Cast a reflex of comfort
    Alike over all.

In his arm-chair sat uncle
    Content as could be,
With the *Albany Journal*
    Spread out on his knee,
And he beamed o'er his spectacles

On the gay crowd;

Took his pipe from his mouth,

And shook hands as we bowed.

We played blindman's buff,

Ate nuts and pop corn—

The happiest children

That ever were born.

Charles told of adventures

By sea and by land,

And we listened in silence,

A wondering band.

The wind now arose;

And the roar of the blast

Made us draw 'round the fire

To wait till 'twas past.

Maple sugar in a kettle

   Was hung on the crane.

Then little recked we

   Of the storm or the rain.

The candy was poured

   On a great cake of ice—

Was ever the like .

   So delicious and nice!

The wind-storm blew louder;

   The sleet and the rain

Pattered down on the roof,

   And shook each window pane.

The tall clock struck midnight—

"Merrie Christmas!" shout all,
For our aunt said, "To-night,
   None depart for the Hall."
Each lighted his candle,
   And with kiss and good-night,
We retired to our rooms
   To rest till daylight.
My sister and I chose
   The curled maple bed,
With the blue plaited canopy
   Over its head.
The curtains were chintz,
   Where the hounds on fox-chase
Were with hunters on horseback

Pursuing the race.

These I often, for hours,

   With wonder admired,

And of subject and figures

   I never grew tired.

One sounded a horn,

   His gun slung by his side;

Others leaped over fences,

   Or ditch long and wide.

We mutter our prayers,

   Ere asleep we now fall,

And we think of our stockings

   At home on the wall;

When faint from afar

Came the sound of a horn—
Had the stage-coach passed by,
    Ere the breaking of morn?
But nearer it came,
    Borne on wings of the blast,
Till close to the gateway
    It sounded at last.
Then a knock—a low voice
    Was now heard, and a moan,
That had moved any heart
    That was not made of stone.
I arose, dressed in haste,
    And opened the door,
And there stood St. Nicholas,

Just as of yore,

With his white beard and pipe,

And his monstrous great sack

Full of drums, dolls and trumpets,

Strapped well on his back.

He entered, all shivering

And trembling, and cold;

And he looked pale and ghastly,

And feeble and old.

He threw down his pack,

And dropped down by the fire,

And gasped, as if ready

At once to expire.

The yule-log still flickered;

The embers I stirred.

He gazed at me now,

And said never a word.

I lighted a lamp,

And brought him some wine.

He leaned on his elbow,

And made me a sign.

He told me his story

In accents all broken;

And his Will to his children

· He left as a token.

" My sleigh was upset

On an icy snow drift;

My reindeer broke loose,

And have left me to shift

In the wind and the sleet

Of this cold winter night;

And I've wandered around

Till this house came in sight.

Now, spent by my toils,

My labors are past—

I have made my lone journey

To die here at last.

This land has great mountains

Of silver and gold,

Such as tales of

Arabian Nights never told.

India's riches no longer

Suffice to supply

Christmas presents—nor gifts

For my children to buy.

Times and manners have changed,

Wealth 's increased, luxury spread;

And 'tis time, like my fathers,

To rest with the dead.

Will you, my dear child,

My testament write,

Set down the last words

Of my Will, here, to-night?

Take down the great ink-horn

From off the high shelf,

And a leaf from the Ledger

Is surely no pelf."

"My blessing to children
    All over the earth,
Whose stockings I've filled
    Since the days of their birth.
Let these children henceforth
    For their children a tree
Of evergreen raise,
    In remembrance of me.
Let them fill it with gifts
    For their households—the poor—
With a dole for the beggar
    That calls at each door.

Let my effigy stand

On the uppermost bough

The Genius of Christmas

Forever, as now."

His voice now grew fainter—

St. Nicholas smiled—

"Make the sign of the Cross—

Write Xmas, my child."

He stretched out his hand

To subscribe to the Will,

But his cold fingers stiffened—

His great heart grew still.

His eyes softly closed,

And he lay back his head,

And I saw good St. Nicholas

Wan, cold, and dead.

My aunt stirred the curtains:

I opened my eyes,

And met her sweet smile

With a look of surprise.

"The breakfast is served,

You alone we await;

Hasten now, to get ready,

Or you 'll be too late."

" And is it not true

That St. Nicholas 's dead?"

Said I, lifting the counterpane,
  Raising my head.

"I think," said Herbert, "that a tree,
  Hung all about with toys,
Would make a very pretty show
  For all the girls and boys."
"I knew 'twas all a dream," said Houghton,
  "For every Christmas night
I've hung my stocking on the wall,
  And had it filled up quite."

Dream "of such stuff as dreams are made,"
  Inwardly to myself I said:

Our grandsire oft in visions saw

    The future all unfold;

And with prophetic word and look,

    Its scenes has oft foretold:

And I possess this instinct fine,

    And presage often feel

As deep, indelibly engraved,

    As writ by pen of steel.

"Now, boys, 'tis time you all retire;

    Lay down your tired heads;

St. Nicholas, when he arrives,

    Must find you in your beds."

So, with "good-night," and hearty kiss,

    We leave the roguish dears,

To sleep in peace till Christmas dawns—
  Which flying time soon nears.

We pass into the kitchen,
  And find before the fire
Master George, with jack-knife, making
  A graven image dire:
He has hollowed out a pumpkin,
  And cut out nose and eyes,
And with a lighted candle,
  Anticipates surprise.

Devillo enters from without,
  Clad for a frosty night,

And opening wide his lantern's door,

    Blows out the shining light.

True guardian of the fold and stalls—

    He 's filled the racks with hay,

That horses, oxen, cows and sheep,

    May have their holiday.

For he has read, on Christmas night

    To dumb brutes speech is given,

That all God's creatures may rejoice

    On earth with those in heaven.

On a foot-stool sits Patsy Bloom,

    In the warm chimney corner:

She 's eating Christmas pie with plums,

Like little Jacky Horner.

The Doctor found her in a hut,

Its shivering inmates chilled

With biting cold and icy blasts,

That every crevice filled.

He wrapped her in a robe of fur,

And brought her to his wife

To warm, and clothe, and cherish her,

And brighten her young life.

"We'll keep her, Ma, through this cold time,

Until there comes a thaw."

And here she sits, nor heeds the wind,

Nor cold, nor weather raw.

The cat is purring by her side,

The ruddy fire-light streams,
And Caper lies upon a rug,
    And growls low in his dreams.

Two younger Maries, with a grave
    And very important air,
Are helping Norah to arrange
    The good, substantial fare.
Rosy-cheeked apples mixed with green,
    All sorts of nuts and cake,
And cider, wine, and steaming punch,
    Will cheerful spirits make.
But the chief sight that greets our eyes
    Is a long line 'gainst the wall,

From which hang stockings ready, now,

 For Santa Claus's call.

Can the old fellow make his way

 Down such a chimney, roaring

With blazing fire from hickory logs,

 Up which the flames are soaring!

"Faith can move mountains," children know;

 Santa Claus, with his pack,

Will surely find his way within

 Through chimney, door, or crack.

Our visit to the kitchen ended,

 The children fast asleep,

We look out of the window,

And see the snow piled deep;

And earth, fence, tree and roof,

In light of the full moon,

Glitter and sparkle in the night

Like gems in rays of noon.

The silver fleeces on the trees,

That look so white and cold,

Are all illusive—all a myth—

Like Jason's fleece of gold.

The stage, on runners, from the East,

Is coming down the hill;

We hear the blast of driver's horn

In the frosty evening still,

And the runners creaking in the snow,

As the stage comes rushing on—
And the horses' speed increases,
  For they know the goal is won.

How speeds the time in leafy Hall,
  Under the evergreens?
Let 's join the merry company,
  And view the festal scenes.
Some at the tables deal out cards;
  Two sit at chess apart;
Others are talking politics,
  And earnest glances dart.
Of slavery, speak in warning words,
  In which sound "wrong" and "right,"

As if the subject soon might breed

    A civil war or fight.

We join a group, playing "Old Maid"—

    Game with a fatal card;

And with whole heart we enter in

    'Gainst the last queen to guard.

Just as the old maid falls to Martha,

    Norah comes walking in

With plates and napkins—too late now

    A new game to begin.

The guests around the tables,

    The circles open wider;

The young folks Philopenas eat,

    The younger ones drink cider.

And thus the hours soon speed away,
    And midnight now draws near,
And Christmas chimes upon the clock
    In tones of loving cheer.
With hearty wishes to each guest,
    "Merrie Christmas, one and all,"
The guests depart, and leave behind
    Silence in Branksome Hall.

My lay is of old fashioned days,
    Ere luxury's prodigal hand
Corruption and folly's seeds had sown
    Broadcast throughout the land.
Ere a new race of paupers came

And filled the land with tramps,

And civil war demoralized

With license of the camps.

In these good days men slept in peace,

Secure with doors unbarred,

Nor life nor property must each

With constant vigil guard.

Then each man sought with honest toil

To earn his daily bread;

And labor done, conscience at rest,

He slept in peaceful bed.

These days were filled with usefulness—

Each helped his suffering brother;

The country's rights and wrongs none left
    To be righted by another.
And here my truthful tale I end
    Of the good old-fashioned times——
Of the early ways and customs
    Told in plain, old-fashioned rhymes.

Lightning Source UK Ltd.
Milton Keynes UK
UKOW07f0825260515

252278UK00011B/443/P